P9-CQQ-353

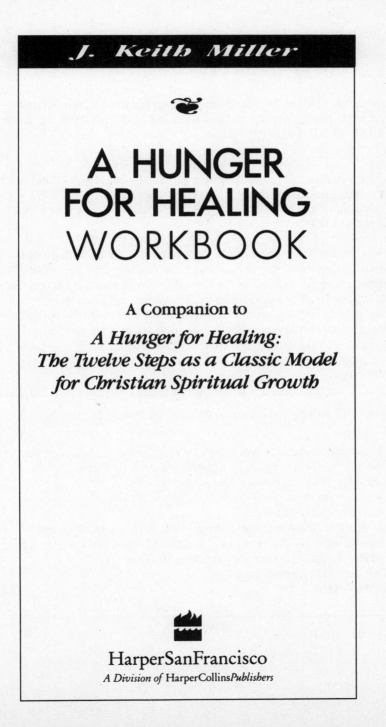

J. Keith Miller

A HUNGER
FOR HEALING
WORKBOOK

A Companion to

*A Hunger for Healing:
The Twelve Steps as a Classic Model
for Christian Spiritual Growth*

HarperSanFrancisco
A Division of HarperCollinsPublishers

To contact J. Keith Miller about speaking engagements, write or call Michael McKinney, McKinney Associates, Inc., P.O. Box 5162, Louisville, KY 40205 phone 1 (502) 583-8222.

Unless otherwise indicated, scripture quotations contained herein are from the Revised Standard Version of the Bible, copyrighted 1946, 1952, 1971 by the Division of Christian Education of the National Council of Churches of Christ in the U.S.A.

A HUNGER FOR HEALING WORKBOOK. Copyright © 1992 by J. Keith Miller. Adapted from *A Hunger for Healing*. Copyright © 1991 by J. Keith Miller. All rights reserved. Printed in the United States of America. No part of this book may be used or reproduced in any manner whatsoever without written permission except in the case of brief quotations embodied in critical articles and reviews. For information address HarperCollins Publishers, 10 East 53rd Street, New York, NY 10022.

FIRST EDITION

Library of Congress Cataloging-in-Publication Data

Miller, Keith.
    A hunger for healing workbook : a companion to A hunger for healing : the Twelve Steps as a classic model for Christian spiritual growth / J. Keith Miller. — 1st ed.
        p.   cm.
    ISBN 0-06-065721-9
    1. Spiritual life—Anglican authors.   2. Twelve-step programs—Religious aspects—Christianity.   3. Spiritual exercises.
I. Miller, Keith.   Hunger for healing.   II. Title.
BV4501.2.M4794   1991 Suppl.
248.8'6—dc20   92-3162
                                                                  CIP

99 RRD-H 10 9 8 7

CONTENTS

HOW TO USE THIS BOOK

*It is the pain of living that creates a hunger
for healing that only God can satisfy.*

Background reading:
A Hunger for Healing, pages 2–9.

In A *Hunger for Healing* I described the ways in which the Twelve-Step program offers a new model for Christian discipleship and spiritual maturity. I firmly believe that the Twelve Steps are a gift that can help all of us, even those free of evident addiction, to be changed by a loving, supportive God who guides us through the pain, anxiety, and confusion of our lives and shows us how to go beyond our own selfish agendas and live a meaningful life seeking God's will. In that book, I tried to take readers inside the spiritual process of each of the Twelve Steps to taste the healing, growing experience of surrendering ourselves to a Higher Power—to us Christians, the God of Jesus Christ.

This workbook is designed as a companion to that effort. The Twelve Steps cannot be "worked" overnight, nor can they be hurried. The self-transformation that the process entails requires a slow, careful program of prayer, meditation, study, introspection, reflection, and action. The exercises and forms provided in this workbook, in conjunction with the reading you'll do in *A Hunger for Healing*, will guide you slowly, carefully, and thoughtfully along the path of spiritual growth. Although this workbook is designed as a private guide, it is in *no way* intended to replace or lessen one's participation in the loving community provided by meetings with others on the way to recovery and a deeper relationship with God. In fact, many will find it helpful to work these steps as a part of a group gathered for that purpose.

Having said that, it is also true that experience indicates that ultimately each person will have to go through the steps at her or his own pace. Thoroughness is important. Speed and competitiveness are often indications of the disease.*

I want to state very clearly that there is not a prescribed "correct" way to take the Twelve Steps. Each pilgrim must make many decisions about the best way for him or her. The material in this workbook and in my previous book comes from many sources and was filtered through my own life and experience while working the steps and working with others in the program.

---

*A complete program to support groups' use of this material has been developed by NavPress. It includes a series of videotapes and a leader's guide. For information about a video-based version of *A Hunger for Healing,* call 1 (800) 366-7788 or write NavPress, P.O. Box 35001, Colorado Springs, CO 80935.

THE TWELVE STEPS AND TWELVE TRADITIONS

The Twelve Steps of Sinners Anonymous*

1. We admitted we were powerless over our Sin—that our lives had become unmanageable.

2. Came to believe that a Power greater than ourselves could restore us to sanity.

3. Made a decision to turn our will and our lives over to the care of God as we understood him.

4. Made a searching and fearless moral inventory of ourselves.

5. Admitted to God, to ourselves, and to another human being the exact nature of our wrongs.

---

* Reprinted with adaptations, and below, with permission of Alcoholics Anonymous World Services, Inc.:

The Twelve Steps as they appear in the Alcoholics Anonymous Big Book are: (1) We admitted we were powerless over alcohol—that our lives had become unmanageable. (2) Came to believe that a Power greater than ourselves could restore us to sanity. (3) Made a decision to turn our will and our lives over to the care of God as we understood him. (4) Made a searching and fearless moral inventory of ourselves. (5) Admitted to God, to ourselves, and to another human being the exact nature of our wrongs. (6) Were entirely ready to have God remove all these defects of character. (7) Humbly asked him to remove our shortcomings. (8) Made a list of all persons we had harmed, and became willing to make amends to them all. (9) Made direct amends to such people wherever possible, except when to do so would injure them or others. (10) Continued to take personal inventory and, when we were wrong, promptly admitted it. (11) Sought through prayer and meditation to improve our conscious contact with God as we understood him, praying only for knowledge of his will and the power to carry that out. (12) Having had a spiritual awakening as the result of these steps, we tried to carry this message to alcoholics and to practice these principles in all our affairs.

6. Were entirely ready to have God remove all these defects of character.

7. Humbly asked him to remove our shortcomings.

8. Made a list of all persons we had harmed, and became willing to make amends to them all.

9. Made direct amends to such people wherever possible, except when to do so would injure them or others.

10. Continued to take personal inventory and, when we were wrong, promptly admitted it.

11. Sought through prayer and meditation to improve our conscious contact with God, praying only for knowledge of his will for us and the power to carry that out.

12. Having had a spiritual awakening as the result of these steps, we tried to carry this message to others and to practice these principles in all our affairs.

The Twelve Traditions of A.A.*

1. Our common welfare should come first: personal recovery depends upon A.A. unity.

2. For our group purpose there is but one ultimate authority—a loving God as He may express Himself in our group conscience. Our leaders are but trusted servants; they do not govern.

3. The only requirement for A.A. membership is a desire to stop drinking.

4. Each group should be autonomous except in matters affecting other groups or A.A. as a whole.

5. Each group has but one primary purpose—to carry its message to the alcoholic who still suffers.

6. An A.A. group ought never endorse, finance, or lend the A.A. name to any related facility or outside enterprise, lest problems of money, property and prestige divert us from our primary purpose.

---

* The Twelve Traditions are reprinted with permission of Alcoholics Anonymous World Services, Inc.

7. Every A.A. group ought to be fully self-supporting, declining outside contributions.

8. Alcoholics Anonymous should remain forever nonprofessional, but our service centers may employ special workers.

9. A.A., as such, ought never be organized; but we may create service boards or committees directly responsible to those they serve.

10. Alcoholics Anonymous has no opinion on outside issues; hence the A.A. name ought never be drawn into public controversy.

11. Our public relations policy is based on attraction rather than promotion; we need always maintain personal anonymity at the level of press, radio, and films.

12. Anonymity is the spiritual foundation of all our traditions, ever reminding us to place principles before personalities.

STEP ONE

We Admitted We Were Powerless over Our Sin—That Our Lives Had Become Unmanageable

A biblical experience of Step One:

*I do not understand my own actions.
For I do not do what I want, but I do the
very thing I hate. . . . I can will what is right,
but I cannot do it. For I do not do the good
I want, but the evil I do not want is what
I do. Now if I do what I do not want, it is
no longer I that do it, but sin which dwells
within me.* (Romans 7:15–20)

Background reading:
A Hunger for Healing, pages 12–27.

Step One has to do with our inherent fear of turning loose our control over ourselves, others, and our futures enough to admit our own weakness and inability to "fix" life and to change the people, places, and things around us. Paradoxically, it is only as we turn loose that we can get free and, like a bumblebee, airborne—in our case, with God.

It seems to be a bedrock truth that we cannot get this spiritual freedom and strength until we can see our own human limitations and quit struggling to "do it ourselves." It seems to us that we have the power; we can do it—even though those of us who are Christians "give God the credit" when we talk about such things. We don't know that this is a delusion until people important to us begin to rebel, and our control is seen to be very limited or illusory.

Our denial, which hides our controlling ways from us, leads us to blame others for our unhappiness and to criticize them. And frequently that blaming and criticism are our escape, our way of not facing the things inside us that lead to our unhappiness and our way of avoiding the awareness that we may be powerless to "fix" everyone and be happy.

The doorway to healing through the Twelve Steps involves the same secret Jesus talked about when he said that "He who loses his life for my sake will find it" (Matt. 10:39). We give up our delusionary control in order to gain a reality-oriented self-control. His "follow me" adventure began with a turning-loose process amazingly like Step One.*

---

*Note: If you are seriously considering taking the Twelve Steps for your own recovery and spiritual growth, you may want to stop at this point and read appendix A on "Sponsorship" in *A Hunger for Healing* (pp. 219–33). It is crucial to a successful Twelve-Step program to have a mentor, or "sponsor," to guide you through the process of taking the steps. This is a New Testament principle that many people are finding essential to authentic spiritual growth. Note how Paul and Barnabas took Silas, Timothy, and Mark and were mentors to them in the faith. (See Acts 15:39–16:5.)

Taking Step One

Continual or Excessive Feelings over Which I Am Powerless

1. Describe your recurring fears (e.g., about finances, family members, authority figures, sex, God).

2. Describe resentments or anger (e.g., about family members, job, government, church, other institutions and people).

3. Describe guilt or shame (e.g., about specific past actions, not being perfect in some area or appearance or performance).

4. Describe sadness or self-pity about at least three things.

5. Describe pain about three situations, people, or thoughts.

6. Describe jealousy (e.g., about material things, abilities, love relationships).

7. Describe how frantic excitability manifests itself in you.

8. Describe how loneliness feels.

9. Describe in what areas you experience numbness or lack of feelings (or confusion) and how these feel.

10. Describe distressing physical symptoms over which you are powerless (e.g., indigestion and/or upset stomach, allergies, trouble sleeping, headaches, skin disorders, muscle or bone problems, sexual dysfunction).

Behaviors over Which I Am Powerless

1. List foods, drinks, medicines that you keep eating, drinking, or taking even though you do not want to.

2. List and describe other compulsive behaviors—things that you keep doing though you know it is not in your best interest to do so. These may include sexual behavior (e.g., excessive masturbation or use of pornography and/or sexual fantasies, having affairs, continual or excessive demands on your partner for sex), gambling or taking risks you can't afford, exaggerating stories, making excuses, lying, justifying yourself (give examples), giving advice or controlling where people don't want you to.

People over Whom I Am Powerless

1. List the people (a) in your family, (b) at work, (c) at church and other places whose behavior irritates you and what it is they do that you can't get them to quit doing.

Summary Statement and Taking the Step

If after considering the issues set out in the past few pages, you can see that in fact you are powerless and that in one or more areas your life is unmanageable, then you may be ready to take Step One.

If you are ready to admit your powerlessness, you can do it by writing out the following statement and/or telling it to your sponsor or the members of a Twelve-Step meeting (if you have no sponsor).

"I, _____ , admit that I am powerless and that my life has become unmanageable."

Write this statement below, using it as it is or putting it in your own words (being sure to use the words *powerless* and *unmanageable*).

You have now taken Step One. It will be helpful to you and others in the program if you will begin to share in meetings some of the ways in which you have discovered that you are powerless. This will help you find the reality and humility essential for progress and may help others to see their own denial and powerlessness so they too can begin this phase of their spiritual journey. If there is something that seems too "shameful" or threatening to share in a meeting, don't share it. Or you may want to talk with your sponsor before sharing it. The idea is not to become a "stripper," but to begin owning and sharing your reality as a part of the healing process.

STEP TWO

*Came to Believe That a Power
Greater Than Ourselves Could
Restore Us to Sanity*

A biblical experience of the power of
coming to believe:

*And the blind man said to him, "Master, let
me receive my sight." And Jesus said to him,
"Go your way; your faith has made you
well." (Mark 10:51, 52)*

A biblical experience of being
restored to sanity:

*And they came to Jesus and saw the demoniac
sitting there, clothed and in his right mind,
the man who had had the legion [of demons].*
(Mark 5:15)

Background reading:
A Hunger for Healing, pages 32–41.

In Step One, we admitted we are powerless, but that leaves us with a terrible void. Knowing our best efforts won't solve our deepest problems, what can we do? The second Step says that there is a Higher Power, a power greater than you that can overcome your disease and help you envision life as it can be lived.

People with all kinds of beliefs about God walk up to this second Step. They have in common only an awareness that they are trapped by an addiction or the Sin-disease and cannot "manage" their lives. Step Two says that after admitting one's powerlessness, all that is required to begin this faith journey is a willingness to believe—no content, no creed, no church affiliation, no religious experience, just a willingness, a sense of openness to a "Higher Power." Hearing this is often very disturbing to Christians, who think that the spiritual life begins with a willingness to believe in Jesus Christ. But a little thought reveals that long before a person makes a specific commitment to Christ there has been some sort of awakening of the desire to believe. Authentic Christian conversion is similar to joining a Twelve-Step group, in the sense that first comes the awareness of one's powerlessness to solve the most basic problems one is facing. Then, perhaps, one meets a loving Christian, hears a speaker, reads a book, or sees a movie in which faith plays a part.

The creative and healing power released by the simple shift from the self-willed, self-centered "I'll do it myself, thank you" attitude of the Sin-disease to the belief that a Higher Power can give us perspective and strength to solve our problems is so great that the very act of believing often relieves the confusion and fear temporarily and moves us into the process of healing.

Taking Step Two

If you are interested in proceeding with Step Two, the first act is to ask yourself if you are willing to believe in a Higher Power, a power greater than yourself that can help you. You may not be able to describe or put a name to the Higher Power (if you are a Christian you may have no problem with this), but the question here is, Because of what I have seen and heard from the people in this program who do believe and are becoming more nearly whole and free people, am I willing to accept the hypothesis that there is a Higher Power who can help me?

If the answer is yes, write out a statement to that effect below. This may sound simplistic and unnecessary, but in the Twelve Steps, thoughts that do not become objective actions don't seem to help much. Because I am a Christian, my own statement might read, "I, Keith Miller, am willing to believe in a Higher Power who can help me. For me, that Higher Power is the God of Jesus Christ."

Write your statement here:

Now you have taken the first half of Step Two. To continue, read and do what follows.

"Came to believe that a Power greater than ourselves could restore us to sanity." On the following pages are listed some behaviors that do not fit the dictionary definition of sanity: "to be free from hurt or disease; having mental faculties in such condition as to be able to anticipate and judge the effects of your actions on other people" and "being without delusions or prejudices . . . 'wise.'"

If you want to finish taking Step Two, describe or give an example of how each of the following dysfunctional and self-defeating behaviors operates in your life (asking how "sane" these behaviors are).

1. In what areas (i.e., personal, vocational, faith, etc.) do you have recurring fears that aren't grounded in sound evidence?

2. Whom do you continue to resent periodically or constantly, and how does your resentment manifest itself? How does it feel?

3. What self-defeating behaviors do you continue to engage in even though it is not in your best interests to continue (e.g., overeating, using drugs or alcohol, entering destructive relationships, gambling, compulsive talking, procrastination)?

4. Give examples of decisions you have made or things you have done that were "crazy"—that is, things you did even though you knew the consequences could be harmful to you (personal/sexual, financial, relational, emotional, etc.).

5. Give examples of not going to get help when you needed it or putting off going (e.g., medical/dental care or counseling help with compulsive-addictive problems, control-Sin-relationship problems).

6. When you see that your self-defeating behavior is insane and you believe that a Higher Power (God) can restore you to sanity, it is helpful to write it out. My statement might be, "I can see that my self-defeating behavior and my refusal to get help to change what I am doing is a form of insanity, and I believe that God can restore me to sanity."

Write your statement in your own words.

STEP THREE

*Made a Decision to Turn Our Will
and Our Lives over to the Care of
God as We Understood Him*

Biblical expressions of the principles
of Step Three:

*You shall love the Lord your God with all
your heart, and with all your soul, and with
all your mind, and with all your strength.*
(Mark 12:30)

*They left the boat and their father,
and followed him.* (Matthew 4:22)

Background reading:
A Hunger for Healing, pages 46–54; 235–44.

The first three steps constitute the beginning of a lifelong turning process in which we change the direction of our lives from the way we think they should go (in our stress and Sin) to the way God thinks they should go, in serenity, humility, and loving obedience to his will as we begin to determine it beyond our denial.

But this idea of surrendering, of releasing authority and control of outcomes to another, is a very difficult notion for thinking persons. Not only does surrendering go against all our childhood injunctions of "do it yourself" and "don't give up," but as long as we can keep our minds churning, we can keep from facing and understanding our own part in causing our painful feelings.

In taking Step Three, you make a decision to turn your will and life over to God, but you don't complete the transaction when you say the words of commitment. Once you decide to give your life and will to him, the other steps are designed to remove the blocks, the things that keep you from surrendering your bruised, self-defeating past and becoming the person God made you to be. Steps Four through Twelve slowly reveal to you the things that have always kept you from being happy and free, from having good boundaries, from being creative and loving, and from doing God's will, and they show you how to surrender these things to God.

If you have decided to work the Twelve Steps and are contemplating doing Step Three, it is very important to realize that if you give up controlling those around you, one or more of them may step into the power void and attempt to control you. Because this is often true, it is important to learn about how you may develop healthy "boundaries" to protect yourself from being controlled and to keep you from inadvertently controlling others.

I have described what boundaries are and how they may be used to help one in recovery in appendix B of *A Hunger for Healing* (pp. 235–44), and I suggest that if you are working the Twelve Steps, you stop and read that material before taking Step Three.

Taking Step Three

A Look at Your Own Background

1. Can you remember being given the following kinds of messages? "Take care of yourself." "Don't bother other people with your problems." "Don't give up." If so, describe the way you remember getting those "do it by yourself" messages. What were the circumstances?

2. What do you feel when you consider really putting your life and your will, your whole future, in God's hands? Fear, excitement, joy, desire to leave the program? Describe your feelings about doing this.

3. What are the specific fears that come to mind when you consider taking Step Three? What might happen to you? What might God do to you? (Or what natural consequences might God allow to happen if you "give up control"?)

4. What kinds of boundaries did your parents help you develop (none, damaged, walls, or intact)? Describe the way you experience boundaries or lack of boundaries in your relationships.

5. Can you believe that God can help you develop healthy boundaries if you turn your life and your will over to him? (If you happen to have been raised in a church that violated your boundaries, you will want to distinguish between turning your life over to God and turning your life over to the Church.) Imagine and describe a scene in which you have good boundaries with someone whom you cannot now stop from putting you down or hurting your feelings.

6. Can you see how turning your life and your will over to God could help you say no to people and circumstances that are not good for you? (Give examples regarding your family, vocation, social life, and personal growth and development.)

God as I Understand Him

1. Can you think of areas in which you do not trust God (e.g., finances, family matters, intimate needs)? List them here. (A way to tell what these areas are is to ask yourself what you worry about a lot.)

2. Can you see the roots of any of these areas of fear and lack of trust in God in your childhood relationship with parents? Describe these beginnings, if possible.

3. If after doing this exercise you feel uneasy, you may want to discuss the things you discovered with your sponsor or a counselor. This exercise is not to try to blame anyone for anything but to see if your fear of surrendering may have its root in a skewed view of God, an unconscious identification of him with your imperfect parents (and all parents are imperfect). You may want to "journal" here about what comes to your mind when you consider these ideas.

4. Have you used God as a servant to do things you ask for and been disappointed when he hasn't done them? Give some examples if possible.

Making the Decision!

If you have already made a commitment of your life to God or Jesus Christ, are you ready now to put your life and your will in his hands to do the changing you'll need to do to defeat the compulsive and painful results of the Sin-disease in your life? If you are ready to make this decision, here is the commitment prayer from A.A.'s Big Book (p. 63) that has served as a model for many people:*

> God, I offer myself to Thee—to build with me and do with me as Thou wilt. Relieve me of the bondage of self, that I may better do Thy will. Take away my difficulties, that victory over them may bear witness to those I would help of Thy Power, Thy love, and Thy way of life. May I do Thy will always.

If you are ready to make this decision, you may want to write out your own commitment prayer below, or if the prayer from the Big Book says it for you, memorize it, copy it, or make it your own by changing or adding to it in any ways that feel right for your situation.

---

*The Big Book is what A.A. members call *Alcoholics Anonymous* (New York: Alcoholics Anonymous World Services, 1986).

STEP FOUR

Made a Searching and Fearless Moral Inventory of Ourselves

Some biblical expressions of the need to deal
with our inventory material:

*If we say we have no sin, we deceive
ourselves, and the truth is not in us.
If we confess our sins, he is faithful
and just, and will forgive our sins and
cleanse us from all unrighteousness.*
(1 John 1:8–9)

*Rend your hearts and not your
garments.* (Joel 2:13)

Background reading:
A Hunger for Healing, pages 60–82.

What we have done in the first three steps is to get in touch with God in a way that allows us to access his power in overcoming Sin and its consequences in our lives. Working Step Four can be the beginning of lasting character changes. We've committed our lives and our will to God to the extent we can, and now we are going to clean house spiritually to find out why we are at war within ourselves and with the people close to us. By doing the next few steps we can uncover denied Sin-behaviors and character defects that have blocked our spiritual growth. The fourth Step tells us how to begin to get at the specific character defects that cripple us, the character defects that because of denial we have trouble even seeing as ours. In Step Four we compile a "moral" inventory—a list of traits and behaviors that have transgressed our highest, or moral, values. We also inventory our "good" traits and the behaviors that represent them. In this moral inventory of our lives, the defects or dysfunctional behaviors might include some that once worked; some dysfunctional behaviors may have saved our lives as children, but they are now out-of-date, self-defeating, and cause us a great deal of trouble when we use them as adults (e.g., tantrums, or making the "grand exit" to avoid facing painful encounters).

Guidelines for Working Step Four

Understand the purposes of Step Four: (1) to acquire deeper self-knowledge that can lead (by continuing in the Twelve Steps) to self-acceptance and even self-love; (2) to face the truth about our behavior; and (3) to identify our behavior patterns so that we are prepared to surrender them and ask God to act in our behalf to make lasting changes in us.

- Expect to rely on a Higher Power to do Step Four.
- Feel your feelings as you go.
- Get the support of a sponsor.
- Attend meetings regularly.
- Banish the myth that you should have been perfect.
- Resist the urge to focus on what others have done to you.
- Write your inventory in the space provided in this workbook, using extras pages if necessary.
- Don't rush; Step Four takes time.

Taking Step Four

There are many approaches to taking Step Four. Several are described here, but no one is expected to do all these things. Each person taking the steps is advised to decide, with the help of a sponsor, how he or she will approach Step Four and how much detail will be included. As you approach the beginning of your own "searching and fearless moral inventory," start at whatever level you can. Let's say you can't think of anything harmful or abusive you've done to others, but in spite of your efforts to resist, you find yourself absorbed with what people have done to you. You might decide to list these problems of others. Whatever you can think of, get it down on paper. Even that much will help, because when you take that list to the fifth Step you will have somebody around to give you feedback and help you interpret what you have written. Most of us, however, will be able to think of specific things we have done sometime in our lives to hurt others.

Resentments

Resentment is the result of a collision between our actions, fed by our swollen instincts, and either the actions of other people or our own highest values. If you are a person who expresses your resentment openly, you may have had some violent feelings or may have taken violent action. Any incidents you can recall should be listed in your inventory, along with a description of the situation. Often, facing these resentments in Step Four relieves one of having to be violent or have crippling feelings later.

Try to recall and write about incidents that may have happened clear back in childhood. These include resentments of people (relatives, friends, or enemies), of institutions (schools, churches, the government, and so on), and of principles by which you have lived.

The inventory begins with a list of the incidents we can recall that created resentment in us. The Big Book (pp. 64 and 71) suggests that you write these resentments in three columns (or, as in this workbook, three sections):

The person or object of my resentment

What happened to cause the resentment

The effects in my life

I have added a fourth section or column, and I suggest trying to recall what you did before the incident listed as a possible "cause" that may have given rise to the other person's action.

For example:

I am *resentful* at Bill Smith [my partner].

The *cause:* Charging big personal expenses to our partnership account. Bought an airplane and charged it to the company. Does not repay the company and treats the plane as his own property.

The *effect* in my life: resentment, pride, fear (instinct involved: security).

What I did earlier to cause the behavior: Dumped business on Bill during a crisis and went on vacation.

I am *resentful* at my wife.

The *cause:* Judges and nags me. Talks about what an attractive man Bill S. is. Makes jokes about how I snore.

The *effect* in my life: resentment, pride, fear (instincts involved: emotional security, sexual security).

What I did earlier to cause the behavior: Manipulated wife to work for me. Set her up to be with Bill all day.

I am resentful at

The cause

Effect in my life

What I did earlier to cause this behavior

I am resentful at

The cause

Effect in my life

What I did earlier to cause this behavior

I am resentful at

The cause

Effect in my life

What I did earlier to cause this behavior

I am resentful at

The cause

Effect in my life

What I did earlier to cause this behavior

I am resentful at

The cause

Effect in my life

What I did earlier to cause this behavior

I am resentful at

The cause

Effect in my life

What I did earlier to cause this behavior

I am resentful at

The cause

Effect in my life

What I did earlier to cause this behavior

I am resentful at

The cause

Effect in my life

What I did earlier to cause this behavior

Fears

Most fear is because our self-reliance failed and our faith failed and we felt that we were not going to get something we wanted or were going to lose something we had. After listing all the resentments you can remember for your whole life, you then list all the fears that you can remember since childhood. Then ask yourself about each incident, Why was I afraid?

For example:

I am *fearful* of financial failure (to have enough to take care of family obligations and retirement).

The *cause:* I remember my father being afraid when he went broke in the Depression when I was a little boy.

The *effect* in my life: I am afraid to trust God with this area of my life, and I vacillate between criticizing family members when they spend money and overspending myself when things are going well. I lose sleep and become critical of others or spend too much time reviewing my own finances.

I am fearful of

The cause

Effect in my life

I am fearful of

The cause

Effect in my life

I am fearful of

The cause

Effect in my life

I am fearful of

The cause

Effect in my life

I am fearful of

The cause

Effect in my life

Swollen Instincts

After listing your resentments and fears, inventory your specific instincts in the three primary trouble areas: sex, security, and social acceptance. I suggest going back to birth again, although some people just write what they can easily remember, not trying to start at birth.

The more specific you can be, the better. At first a person might try to be too general and say, "Well, I have always had a little problem with the opposite sex." That will not do it. The idea here is to clean house and face the specific ways you have allowed each instinct to get out of proportion because of your self-centeredness in the Sin-disease.

Sexual Instincts   "Sexuality" is not just about being in bed with somebody. Sexuality here includes the nature of the relationships you have had with members of the opposite sex, including but not limited to explicit sexual experiences.

For example:

Behavior: Excessive sexual fantasizing

Attitudes: Leads to shame and guilt feelings and to making depersonalized demands for sex on my spouse

Behavior

Attitudes

Behavior

Attitudes

Behavior

Attitudes

A HUNGER FOR HEALING WORKBOOK

Financial Security   When you inventory your life regarding financial insecurity, ask yourself, What character defects drove me to exaggerate my financial needs so that I got absorbed and obsessed with making money? If you are not absorbed with making money, perhaps it is your spending of it that is out of control. If that is the case, ask yourself, What character defects propel me to spend money beyond my income? Perhaps your problem is the reverse: you have a distinct distaste for or fear of spending money to the point that you and your family are subject to unnecessary deprivation even though your family's income could provide more comforts. Ask yourself what character defects contribute to your need to hoard money, not spending the necessary money to provide for yourself or your family.

Behavior

Attitudes

Behavior

Attitudes

Behavior

Attitudes

Emotional Security   The obsession with emotional security can lead one either to be overdependent and controlled by some stronger person or to start controlling other people in order to feel secure. Either condition often arises from codependence, a very painful "disease."

To inventory your emotional security issues, list all your personal relationships in which there have been recurring emotional problems. Just list every relationship: this child, this friend, my mother, my father, my brother, whomever. Beside each person's name put the feelings that the name calls forth (e.g., pain, fear, anger, shame, guilt, or sadness).

Next, go through the three areas of instinctual need with each person. Is the painful emotion caused by a sexual anxiety or frustration? Is it caused by a financial situation with this person? Is it caused by an exaggerated need for material success? Is it caused by emotional insecurity regarding social needs or sexual passion?

It may seem strange to examine one particular instinct using all three instincts as a guide. But this exercise is to help us break free from our own denial and to begin to become responsible. Writing down our sins and defects in Step Four is a good way to start this process. It's harder to deny your defects after you have written them on a list.

Relationship/Person	Feeling	Cause

Relationship/Person	Feeling	Cause

Social Instincts   With regard to the social instinct, instead of simply wanting to be a regular member of a group, we want to be president of the committee. Or we want to be the smartest, best-looking, holiest, so that we can be considered one of the "special ones." If we become power-mad, we try to control things financially, politically, and socially. We may ruin our chances for intimate personal relationships because we are always jockeying for social position and trying to get someone to do something that will help us fulfill our plans.

To inventory your issues regarding the social instinct, list the social connections you have had that have been painful in some way. Consider whether your pain comes from not receiving a position you wanted, the recognition you believed you deserved, or the attention you wanted. Then list the harmful or dysfunctional things you did as a result. What character defects and feelings were involved in these situations? If none of these fits, then ask yourself why your affiliation with that particular group or organization has been painful.

List the names of any people with whom you have close personal relationships now or have had in the past. If a relationship is over, write about how it ended. Write about any conflicts you had with that person during the relationship. You may begin to see patterns in your past and present relationships.

Positive Traits

When you have finished listing the "damaged goods" in your inventory, take some time to list the positive things that you have realized about your past behavior, character traits, and attitudes since being in the program. For example, "I am an intelligent, sensitive person. I'm a good listener. I am really trying to work this program. I want to learn to do God's will."

STEP FIVE

*Admitted to God, to Ourselves,
and to Another Human Being the
Exact Nature of Our Wrongs*

A biblical expression of the need to do
Step Five with another person, and its
connection with healing:

*Therefore confess your sins to one another,
and pray for one another, that you may
be healed.* (James 5:16)

Background reading:
A Hunger for Healing, pages 86–106.

Even a quick reading of this step reveals that it is a form of confession. This way of confessing is one of the remarkable aspects of the Twelve Steps: the recovery of an incredibly healing and restoring Christian practice.

From the beginning Christians have believed in confessing their sins to other Christians not trained in theology or (more recently) psychology. The author of James stated it clearly as a part of the healing process, "Confess your sins to one another, and pray for one another, that you may be healed" (James 5:15).

Step Four is a way to look at the effects of our swollen instinctual needs for material and emotional security, for sex, and for social acceptance. Step Five can be considered to be a spiritual filter for the toxic memories, thoughts, and behaviors of the past that continue to sabotage and poison our lives and relationships in the present. Just as a kidney dialysis cleanses our blood by filtering the poison from our system and leaving the healthy fluids and tissue to keep cleansing us, Step Five helps us filter out the hidden, crippling behaviors and character defects from the past that are poisoning our relationships with God, with other people, and with ourselves.

The minute people quit defending their image and take Step Five, they often can start being intimate in meetings. They can begin to reveal out loud in front of others something of who they really are today. This kind of honesty turns everything around; the energy once used to enforce denial starts working toward uncovering, discovering the very defects we attempted to hide, and moves us toward honesty instead of toward dishonesty. A person taking Step Five is like a train going into a roundhouse one way and being turned around so it can come back out going in the opposite direction.

Christianity calls this kind of change "repentance" and conversion. Repentance (in Greek, *metanoia*) is a "turning." An army is going one way, and at a signal the army changes direction and goes a different way. The army converts. And in taking Steps One through Five, we change. We start to see our denial, our unreal images, and go in a different direction— toward dismantling our painted facades and becoming the persons God intended us to be. All of the Twelve Steps guide us toward this changing, this going a different direction.

Taking Step Five

The process of taking Step Five has three distinct phases:

1. You choose a person to whom you will admit "the exact nature of your wrongs."
2. You meet with that person and tell him or her what you have learned in Step Four.
3. You listen to any feedback the person you've chosen has for you and take it in.

Your Step Five Record

Be sure to save your written fourth Step and any additional notes you made for your fifth Step. These may be helpful when you take Steps Eight and Nine.

1. The name and phone number of the person you choose to hear your fifth Step:

2. The date of your fifth Step:

3. As you told your fifth Step to your chosen listener, what feelings did you experience?

4. What behavioral or relationship patterns, if any, did you discover during this step?

5. Describe how you feel now after having completed the fifth Step. (Some people have rather dramatic changes in their feelings about themselves, others, God, or life in general. Other people, who work an equally good program, do not have much of an immediate change in feelings.)

STEP SIX

*Were Entirely Ready to Have
God Remove All These
Defects of Character*

Some biblical expressions of the need to be entirely
ready to commit our whole lives to God in
such a complete way that he may transform
not only our character defects but our entire
minds so that we can know and do God's will:

*I appeal to you brethren, by the mercies of
God, to present your bodies as a living
sacrifice, holy and acceptable to God, which
is your spiritual worship. Do not be
conformed to this world but be transformed
by the renewal of your mind, that you may
prove [know] what is the good and acceptable
and perfect will of God. (Romans 12:1–2)*

*Search me, O God, and know my heart!
—Try me and know my thoughts!
And see if there be any wicked way in me,
—And lead me in the way everlasting!*
(Psalm 139:23–24)

Background reading:
A Hunger for Healing, pages 108–13.

As we completed Step Five, many of us experienced a new energy and freedom to begin again. In Steps Six and Seven we are offered something altogether different from the way many of us have been instructed to live in relation to God: an impossible goal—and a way to achieve it.

We have arrived at a crucial and often overlooked spiritual principle of healing and growth. Our part in the removal of our character defects involves a new attitude toward God and how he works to change our lives in the practical struggles of living.

Taking Step Six

1. Consider which religious behaviors you have engaged in that you now realize you used in the hope of fixing yourself (e.g., longer prayer time, more intense Bible study, doing volunteer work). Describe your feelings about doing each of those things at the time (joy, impatience, hope, frustration, boredom, anger, fear, etc.).

2. In what ways have you tried to fix yourself with your own power (e.g., stuffing feelings such as anger to "prove you had faith"; trying harder to resist a temptation or a character defect such as impatience, sarcasm, or resentment; criticizing yourself harshly whenever one of your character defects was active)?

A HUNGER FOR HEALING WORKBOOK

3. What character defects have you recognized that you need to become willing to let God remove?

4. Are there any character defects you have discovered that you enjoy and are not sure you want God to remove—or know you don't want him to remove? If so, name them (e.g., greed, grandiose thinking, lust).

5. Describe how you have attempted to use your own power to fix others (e.g., giving advice, giving them books or tapes they have not asked for so they can get fixed, withholding communication, affection, money, or sex until they do what you "think best").

6. Write in your own words your statement to God that you are now ready for him to remove all your defects of character.

STEP SEVEN

Humbly Asked Him to Remove Our Shortcomings

A biblical expression of the nature of the radical shift that can take place through Step Seven, from an anxious, material, or intellectual faith to a spiritual life of trust in God:

Truly, truly, I say to you, unless one is born anew, he cannot see the kingdom of God. . . . That which is born of the flesh is flesh, and that which is born of the Spirit is spirit. (John 3:3–6)

Background reading:
A Hunger for Healing, pages 116–28.

On completing Step Six, we were on the brink of entering the world of spiritual living, on the brink of growth at new and deeper levels than most of us had ever imagined. Approaching Step Seven we experience at least the beginnings of readiness to let God take over the work of healing us!

Taking Step Seven is for many of us the greatest act of authentic humility we have ever been asked to commit: to transfer control of our recovery to God. Although this step sounds simple at first, it is an amazing spiritual watershed. Where we had once asked God to help us *get* out of our pain and *get* our lives back on track, now we are telling him that at last we are putting ourselves in his hands so completely that we want God to remove any defects that stand in the way of our being the person God wants us to be—letting God decide what these defects are. In a paradoxical way, we are going to quit trying to fix ourselves.

This is the suggested prayer in the Big Book for taking Step Seven the first time: "My Creator, I am now willing that you should have all of me, good and bad. I pray that you now remove from me every single defect of character that stands in the way of my usefulness to you and my fellows. Grant me strength, as I go out from here, to do your bidding. Amen" (p. 76).

Taking Step Seven

1. What does humility mean to you? (If you draw a blank, you may want to read the discussion on pp. 116–17 of *A Hunger for Healing*.)

2. Describe the ways your grandiosity manifests itself in your life. (Here are some examples: thinking if I could just get organized, I could accomplish a superhuman amount; thinking if I pleased my husband or wife enough, he or she would treat me with respect and love; thinking if I stopped being passive and stood up to my wife and "acted like a man," I could heal all the problems in our marriage by myself; thinking if I could send my son enough money, he would eventually get and keep a good job and pay his own way; thinking if I could calmly educate my roommate about the perils of smoking, she would eventually quit.)

A HUNGER FOR HEALING WORKBOOK

3. Write down the date you prayed the Seventh-Step Prayer, or your own version of it.

4. Record what positive character traits could replace your character defects (listed in doing Four, Five, and Six).

For example:

Defect: *Fear*

Positive trait: *Courage*

Defect:

Positive trait:

Defect:

Positive trait:

Defect:

Positive trait:

Defect:

Positive trait:

Defect:

Positive trait:

Defect:

Positive trait:

Defect:

Positive trait:

Defect:

Positive trait:

Defect:

Positive trait:

Defect:

Positive trait:

Defect:

Positive trait:

Defect:

Positive trait:

Defect:

Positive trait:

Note: You may want to make a list of these positive traits and read them aloud to yourself every morning for thirty days. For example:

> I have courage
>
> I am sensitive.
>
> I am able to be on time.

Reading this list aloud or putting it on tape and listening to it for a month are acts of believing that God is able to (and will) change you and your life.

5. As time goes on, you may notice that a character defect has been removed, and you felt or behaved differently in what used to be a painful situation. When you notice this, record these incidents here.

6. After asking God to take their whole lives, some people have found it helpful to begin to get in touch with what they have naturally liked to do, realizing that God also touches us through experiences we are drawn to. Many of us have spent our lives filling roles unnatural to us to win some sort of love or approval, and part of recovery is to find God's will (the way he has made us) for how we are going to spend our vocational and recreational time. If you would like to get in touch with this aspect of your life, you can make a beginning by going back and listing things in your life you have enjoyed doing (e.g., hiking, doing math problems, gardening, writing, teaching).

STEP EIGHT

Made a List of All Persons We Had Harmed, and Became Willing to Make Amends to Them All

A biblical expression of the need to see our own faults, our part, and to forgive those who have hurt us before going out to make amends, hoping for forgiveness:

Why do you see the speck that is in your brother's eye, but do not notice the log that is in your own eye? Or how can you say to your brother, "Let me take the speck out of your eye," when there is a log in your own eye? You hypocrite, first take the log out of your own eye. (Matthew 7:3–5)

Background reading:
A Hunger for Healing, pages 132–44.

We are now at a turning point in the recovery process. The moment we agree to have all our own defects removed (in Step Seven), God turns us outward to prepare us to love others. However, before we can love others in a healthy way in the present, it seems that we must do what we can to heal the broken and bruised relationships of the past. The guilt, shame, pain, and resentment surrounding these relationships we have bungled are stored in the basements of our lives; this putrid, musty, hidden material isolates us and makes us want to keep our distance both from other people and from God. We are afraid of new relationships for fear they will be just as painful, or maybe afraid that if we get too close again people might discover the past results of our Sin and reject us.

As we approach Steps Eight and Nine, it is helpful to remember that in healing bruised relationships it is often necessary to do exactly the opposite of what we feel an urge to do and perhaps what we saw our parents and the elders of the church doing in their meetings and relationships. For example, when we have hurt someone's feelings in our families, our first internal response may be to try to justify ourselves. If that doesn't work, we then often try to bury the incident and pacify the person, perhaps doing something nice to make the person forget our thoughtless or abusive behavior.

But in Steps Eight and Nine we learn that the way out of the pain of separation is *through* that pain, not around it. Instead of justifying ourselves, we own our hurtful behavior specifically. Instead of burying what we find, we go to the person we have offended, confess the behavior, and make amends. When you first read about Steps Eight and Nine it's good to remember that you're supposed to have done Steps One through Seven first, which may have taken you as long as two or three years.

Step Eight is a social housecleaning, just as Step Four was our personal housecleaning. In Step Eight we're setting out to clean up all the bruised relationships and the pockets of guilt, pain, fear, resentment, and sadness that are stored inside, stuck to our shameful past deeds. For this undealt-with material blocks us from loving other people, ourselves, and God in the present.

Taking Step Eight

1. Make a list of people you have harmed. The Twelve and Twelve defines "harm" as "the result of instincts in collision, which cause physical, mental, emotional, or spiritual damage to people" (p. 80).* Each person has to decide when he or she has done harm to another.

Using the forms below, describe briefly what you did. (You might add how you justified doing it.) Then describe the consequences in your relationship with that person, such as any strain or separation between you, and any damages or loss the other person suffered.

People I have harmed:

---

* The "Twelve and Twelve" is *Twelve Steps and Twelve Traditions* (New York: Alcoholics Anonymous World Services, 1983).

Person's name:

What happened? (my harmful behavior):

Consequences (separation and/or damages):

Person's name:

What happened? (my harmful behavior):

Consequences (separation and/or damages):

Person's name:

What happened? (my harmful behavior):

Consequences (separation and/or damages):

Person's name:

What happened? (my harmful behavior):

Consequences (separation and/or damages):

Person's name:

What happened? (my harmful behavior):

Consequences (separation and/or damages):

Person's name:

What happened? (my harmful behavior):

Consequences (separation and/or damages):

Person's name:

What happened? (my harmful behavior):

Consequences (separation and/or damages):

Person's name:

What happened? (my harmful behavior):

Consequences (separation and/or damages):

2. For each of the incidents you have described, write about any feelings you now have concerning your harmful behavior and the consequences.

Person's name:

My feelings today:

Person's name:

My feelings today:

Person's name:

My feelings today:

Person's name:

My feelings today:

Person's name:

My feelings today:

Person's name:

My feelings today:

Person's name:

My feelings today:

Person's name:

My feelings today:

Person's name:

My feelings today:

3. Make a list of the people who have harmed you, what each person did, and how you have felt about it up until now. As you experience the feelings you have had about what these people did to harm you, become aware that the people whom you have harmed have probably had very similar feelings about you.

Person who has harmed me:

What this person did to me:

How I felt about it:

Person who has harmed me:

What this person did to me:

How I felt about it:

A HUNGER FOR HEALING WORKBOOK

Person who has harmed me:

What this person did to me:

How I felt about it:

Person who has harmed me:

What this person did to me:

How I felt about it:

Person who has harmed me:

What this person did to me:

How I felt about it:

4. For each incident listed under item 3 that you would like to get over and drop as an issue between you and the other person, write out a brief statement of forgiveness for that person. If you are not honestly ready to drop one of the incidents you listed, do not write that statement. Just write the ones you can. (This is not to suggest that you go and tell the other person you forgive him or her unless you are *asked* for forgiveness. Your *willingness* to forgive, however, can change *your* life and, in some cases, the relationship.)

Person:

Statement of forgiveness:

Person:

Statement of forgiveness:

Person:

Statement of forgiveness:

Person:

Statement of forgiveness:

Person:

Statement of forgiveness:

Person:

Statement of forgiveness:

Person:

Statement of forgiveness:

5. Write out your statement of readiness to make amends to the people you have harmed. To be rigorously honest, list exceptions, if there are any. If and when you become ready to make amends to the ones you excepted, come back to this page and write out your statement of readiness for each one. When you are willing to make amends to them all, you are ready to take Step Nine.

STEP NINE

*Made Direct Amends to Such
People Wherever Possible,
Except When to Do So Would
Injure Them or Others*

Biblical principles relating to the necessity of
making amends in order to better love God
and other people:

*So if you are offering your gift at the altar,
and there remember that your brother has
something against you, leave your gift there
before the altar and go; first be reconciled
to your brother, and then come and
offer your gift.* (Matthew 5:23–24)

*You shall not hate your brother in your
heart, but you shall reason with your
neighbor, lest you bear sin because of him.
You shall not take vengeance or bear any
grudge against the sons of your own people,
but you shall love your neighbors as
yourself.* (Leviticus 19:17–18)

Background reading:
A Hunger for Healing, pages 148–60.

Making amends is part of the process of reconciliation around which the whole Christian message revolves. Being a Christian does not "require" that we do Step Nine, but unless we take the risk of being rejected and make amends, we do not become reconciled with those we have harmed, and we are blocked not only from relating to those persons but also from worshiping God. Jesus said that even when you are offering your gift at the altar and you remember that you've harmed someone, go right then and be reconciled to that person first and then come to offer your gift.

The Twelve Steps teach us that we can be healed, but that a part of this healing is to take responsibility for our lives and actions. When we make amends we are simply telling the person we harmed the truth about our actions as we now see them, trusting that the healing, the self-acceptance, and the serenity we will gain are worth the rejection we may encounter. We are trusting that God and our fellow seekers in this Way can do more to bring us to happiness and intimacy than any negative opinion could hurt us. Although risking open rejection by those to whom we make amends is frightening, we have the experience of thousands of people who have taken this step before us to encourage and strengthen us as we go. After making amends to all the people we listed in Step Eight, we begin to experience the "promises of the program" (see pp. 158–60 in *A Hunger for Healing*).

Doing Step Nine correctly also takes courage, prudence, good judgment, and a careful sense of timing. If you are just coming into the Twelve Steps as you read this, remember that you're not ready to do Step Nine yet. You've got eight steps to walk through first. By the time you get to this point you may be amazed at the way you have become ready to trust God and do Step Nine.

Taking Step Nine

On the following pages, list the people you want to make amends to in each of the categories below. After you have made each of your amends, write beside that person's name the date and the method by which you made amends (e.g., phone call, personal visit, letter, discussion with your sponsor) as well as your feelings about having made the amends. It is common for one's feelings to become increasingly positive as time elapses.

Group 1:
People you went to right away (people you have already made the initial amends to). Was there any offer of restitution you needed (or need) to make (e.g., pay back money or replace something you broke)?

Name	Date of Amends	Method	Restitution Needed?	Feelings

Name	Date of Amends	Method	Restitution Needed?	Feelings

Group 2:
People to whom you do not think you should make full disclosure.

Name	Date of Amends	Method	Restitution Needed?	Feelings

Name	Date of Amends	Method	Restitution Needed?	Feelings

Group 3:
*Specific amends to family members and close friends,
business amends, amends about money, and so on.*

Name	Date of Amends	Method	Restitution Needed?	Feelings

Name	Date of Amends	Method	Restitution Needed?	Feelings

Group 4:
People with whom you cannot make contact.

Name	Date of Amends	Method	Restitution Needed?	Feelings

Name	Date of Amends	Method	Restitution Needed?	Feelings

A HUNGER FOR HEALING WORKBOOK

Group 5:

People you are not yet willing *to make amends to. (It has been helpful
for many people to put those in this category on a list and pray for them
and their wholeness and welfare until you are ready to make amends.
This may sound impossible, but sometimes it leads to amazing changes
in attitude in the one praying.)*

Name	Date of Amends	Method	Restitution Needed?	Feelings

Name	Date of Amends	Method	Restitution Needed?	Feelings

STEP TEN

Continued to Take Personal Inventory and, When We Were Wrong, Promptly Admitted It

Some biblical expressions of the need to continue to watch for our defects and to search out things that might hinder us so that we won't be tempted and slip, and of the need, if we do slip, to make amends:

Watch and pray that you may not enter into temptation; the spirit is indeed willing but the flesh is weak. (Mark 14:38)

If he turns from his sin and does what is lawful and right, if the wicked restores the pledge, gives back what he has taken by robbery, and walks in the statutes of life, committing no iniquity, he shall surely live, he shall not die. None of the sins that he has committed shall be remembered against him; he has done what is lawful and right, he shall surely live. (Ezekiel 33:14–16)

If we walk in the light, as he is in the light, we have fellowship with one another, and the blood of Jesus his son cleanses us from all sin. (1 John 1:7)

Background reading:
A Hunger for Healing, pages 164–75.

The first nine steps contain the behavioral and spiritual reformation process of the program. The last three steps show the pilgrim how to maintain the new life that comes as a result of committing one's life and will to God, working the steps, and giving away what one is finding.

Step Ten is often considered by newcomers to be a throwaway step. People say, "Well, I'm going to continue the program. There's no need to do anything specific about Step Ten." And they pass over it as if it weren't there. But it's one of the most important steps of all to many of us who have been in the Twelve-Step process awhile.

Step Ten is a spiritual pocket computer to help us keep tabs on our behavior today and a cleanser to help keep our spiritual lenses clean. In this method of keeping an inventory every day, we ask ourselves questions like, Which of my character defects popped up as uninvited guests today? Am I using the tools of the program? Am I praying? Am I thanking God for all the good things he has done for me this day, and for any positive things he's freed me to do? Am I reading the Bible? Am I reading the Big Book? Am I going to my sponsor? Am I going to worship?

The reason this is so important is that the Sin-disease, with its denial and delusion, is always hovering "just a decision away" to throw us back into fear and confusion. In Step Ten we learn to use the first nine steps as spiritual "tools" on a daily basis to keep our lives close to reality, to humility, and to God.

Taking Step Ten

Using the First Three Steps

Note: It is not necessary for everyone to do all of the following to stay in recovery. These are simply suggestions that have helped others.

Did any incidents of conflict occur with anyone today? If so, how can you use the first three steps to regain serenity and clarity so you can decide how to respond?

For each incident, go through the following steps.

Step One: I am powerless over (describe situation or name of person).

Step Two: Describe any "insanity" (thoughts, exaggerated feelings, inappropriate behavior) from which God needs to restore you regarding this incident.

Step Three: Write out your decision to turn whatever you described in Step One over to God.

Incident:

Step One:

Step Two:

Step Three:

Incident:

Step One:

Step Two:

Step Three:

Incident:

Step One:

Step Two:

Step Three:

A HUNGER FOR HEALING WORKBOOK

Incident:

Step One:

Step Two:

Step Three:

Incident:

Step One:

Step Two:

Step Three:

Doing a Spot-Check Inventory

For each incident described, take a spot-check inventory of *your part* in the conflict and make a decision concerning your need to make amends. If you need to do this, go to the person, or make an appointment, and make amends. Describe the results below.

Doing a Daily Inventory

At the end of each day, review your list of character defects and note any examples of them that surfaced during the day so you can make amends tomorrow. The defects listed below are from the Big Book. Disregard any that don't apply to you, and add any of your own that are not included. Use the form below to record one day's inventory.

Character Defect	Example Today	Check When You Have Made Amends Where Appropriate
selfishness		
dishonesty		
resentment		
fear		
jealousy		
self-pity		
greed		
envy		
depression		
hatred		
self-will		
self-reliance		
_____		
_____		
_____		

Doing a Periodic Inventory

1. Gratitude: List all the things you have to be grateful for that have happened since you did your original Step Four inventory (or your last periodic inventory).

2. Consider the decisions you made when you did Step Three. Is there anything in your life today that indicates you may have "taken back" any of the things that you surrendered then or in Step Seven (e.g., addictions, lying, attempts to control or be abusive to a person in a particular situation)? Describe. After you have completed the list, take Step Three again, and turn these specific things over to God.

3. Have you found any new character defects since you took Steps Six and Seven? List them, then work through Steps Six and Seven regarding these newly discovered defects.

4. Are there any bruised relationships in your life for which you have not made amends for your part in the damage? List the person's name, what happened, and the effect in your life. Then work Steps Eight and Nine on each incident. Use the forms below to describe what you did and why you did it, and to characterize the consequences in your relationship with that person.

People I have harmed:

What happened? (my harmful behavior):

Consequences (separation and/or damages):

People I have harmed:

What happened? (my harmful behavior):

Consequences (separation and/or damages):

People I have harmed:

What happened? (my harmful behavior):

Consequences (separation and/or damages):

People I have harmed:

What happened? (my harmful behavior):

Consequences (separation and/or damages):

A HUNGER FOR HEALING WORKBOOK

STEP ELEVEN

Sought Through Prayer and Meditation to Improve Our Conscious Contact with God, Praying Only for Knowledge of His Will for Us and the Power to Carry That Out

Some biblical expressions concerning prayer and meditation, praying for God's will, and the need for help and his power for this area of our lives:

Ask and it will be given you; seek, and you will find; knock, and it will be opened to you. For everyone who asks receives, and he who seeks finds, and to him who knocks it will be opened. (Luke 11:9–10)

Background reading:
A Hunger for Healing, pages 179–93.

Pray then like this:
Our Father who art in heaven,
Hallowed be thy name.
Thy kingdom come,
Thy will be done,
On earth as it is in heaven.
Give us this day our daily bread;
And forgive us our debts,
As we have forgiven our debtors;
And lead us not into temptation,
But deliver us from evil.
For thine is the kingdom and the power
and the glory, for ever. Amen.
(Matthew 6:9–13)

Nevertheless, not as I will,
but as Thou wilt. (Matthew 26:39)

The Spirit helps us in our weakness;
for we do not know how to pray as
we ought, but the Spirit himself intercedes
for us with sighs too deep for words.
(Romans 8:26)

The entire Twelve-Step program is designed to get us out of the "God role" and to put a loving, moral, and forgiving God back in control of our world. When we do this, there is reality and sanity at the center of our lives instead of a flighty, scared person in denial on a search for who knows what that will make him or her happy. For Christians this God is the God of Jesus Christ. But even Christians disagree concerning the appropriate ways to grow spiritually through prayer and meditation. The Twelve Steps provide a simple, direct approach to getting to know God in the context of everyday living.

A HUNGER FOR HEALING WORKBOOK

The Twelve-Step view of what is appropriate and effective in prayer is very different in several important ways from the Christian approach that I grew up with and was trained in. The Twelve and Twelve points out that "prayer is the raising of the heart and mind to God," and the authors include meditation in that (p. 102). There is a sense in which the purpose of prayer and meditation in the program is almost entirely to help us learn how to hear God and to sensitize us to read the signs in our lives and in the world that can guide us toward knowing God and living life as God wants us to. There is very little about asking him to do things we ourselves want done. The strong consensus is that we are so controlling and self-centered and so in denial in our Sin that almost all our requests for ourselves and other people are tainted with the conviction that we know what is best for other people and ourselves—this the program knows to be delusion.

Knowing all this, the founders of A.A. put a clause in Step Eleven that disturbs many Christians who have been praying all their lives: "praying only for knowledge of his will for us and the power to carry that out." It says *only*. I've always had a lot more to tell God about than that. Good Christians have always prayed for some or all of the following: specific answers to our questions, a particular outcome in a specific situation, an end to our pain or our disease (or whatever is causing us trouble), financial success or a certain level of financial security, vocational success—and that God's will be done. The wisdom of the Twelve-Step program, as many of us have discovered, is that most of these prayer subjects are too "dangerous" for our spiritual health. But the experience of many of us is that when we pray for God's will for us and learn to listen for his word on the subject of our lives, we will be given those directions and gifts that are best for our recovery and our happiness.

Taking Step Eleven

1. Find a place and time of day to begin a daily prayer time. Write those below:

2. If having a prayer and meditation time is new to you, describe your difficulties, if any, in doing it (getting too busy, forgetting, and so on).

3. If you already had a prayer and meditation time before beginning these steps, describe any changes you have made in the way you spend this time as a result of working the Twelve Steps. In other words, write out the daily prayer format you are using (or plan to use).

4. If you have become aware of ways you've "played God" through your prayers for yourself or other people, describe them (e.g., asking that people change to suit you, to get well on your timetable, to find a mate).

5. If you have begun to experience what I call nudges (to do certain things) during your prayer time or during the day, list some of these nudges (whether you followed up on them or not).

6. If you have followed up on any of your nudges, what did you do, and what happened to you in the process?

7. What meditation methods have you chosen? Asking for God's will and then listening for a set period of time (e.g., five minutes, ten minutes), writing what comes to you? Saying a word on which to focus? Reading a passage and thinking about it? Describe.

8. If visualization is a helpful thing for you, describe what you are visualizing during your meditation time. A meeting place with God? Yourself healed from character defects?

STEP TWELVE

Having Had a Spiritual Awakening as the Result of These Steps, We Tried to Carry This Message to Others and to Practice These Principles in All Our Affairs

Some biblical principles pertaining to living out Step Twelve:

Therefore, if anyone is in Christ he is a new creation, the old has passed away, behold the new has come. (2 Corinthians 5:17)

Go home to your friends, and tell them how much the Lord has done for you, and how he has had mercy on you. (Mark 5:19)

Teaching them to observe all that I have commanded you; and lo, I am with you always, to the close of the age. (Matthew 28:20)

Background reading:
A Hunger for Healing, pages 196–213.

One of the paradoxical bedrock truths of the Twelve-Step program (and the Christian message) is that we can stay spiritually alive only by giving away what we are receiving. We do this through sharing our experience, strength, and hope as we tell others how we came to the end of ourselves and stepped through powerlessness into the program. We share what is happening to change our lives and give us hope. And we carry the message by helping people who are still hopeless, helpless, and afraid.

Taking Step Twelve

A Spiritual Awakening

Describe below what you believe to be your spiritual awakening. An image that has come to you that gives meaning and hope? New attitudes about God or a feeling of closeness or reality about your faith? New hope about life and relationships? A sense that pain is not the enemy? A realization that you are at last living in reality (and not denial) in some areas of your life?

Carrying the Message

Write the three-part version of your story: (1) what you were like before you came to a Twelve-Step program, including specifically areas in which you were powerless and in denial; (2) what the crisis, or issue of powerlessness, was that brought you to the program and to surrender to God to get help (describe, including your feelings); and (3) what is now different about your life in the same areas you described in part 1. For example, if you were impatient, bossy, and afraid, or if you had a chemical dependency and were in denial, has that changed? How? How has working the program helped you? (What you are doing here is writing in brief form your "story," or, as Christians sometimes call it, your "witness" of what God has done for you. When asked what the Twelve Steps have meant to you, you may want to share this account as your "experience, strength, or hope."

Sponsorship

If someone has asked you to sponsor him or her and you have accepted, write about the experience and feelings you have as you sponsor that person. How is sponsoring someone helping you to work your program? (That is, do you contact your own sponsor more? Go to more meetings? Realize again how much the program and your relationship with God mean to you?)

Practicing the Principles in All Our Affairs

As you now begin to face the issues you used to avoid, what is different about the way you deal with conflict, pain, disappointment, fear, or any other matters that used to trouble you? Write about as many as you wish, but try to describe at least three.

Final note: You may now want to go back and read what you have written in this workbook in order to realize and solidify the many changes in your life you will likely find reflected here. Many of us have found it helpful to do the steps again periodically, since new issues keep arising and coming out of denial in our lives. May this be a wonderful chapter in your life!

Also by J. Keith Miller

The Taste of New Wine

A Second Touch

Habitation of Dragons

The Becomers

The Edge of Adventure (with Bruce Larson)

Living the Adventure (with Bruce Larson)

The Passionate People (with Bruce Larson)

Please Love Me

The Single Experience (with Andrea Miller)

The Scent of Love

The Dream

Hope in the Fast Lane (previously published as *Sin*)

Facing Codependence (with Pia Mellody and Andrea Wells Miller)

Facing Love Addiction (with Pia Mellody and Andrea Wells Miller)

A Hunger for Healing

Compelled to Control

And of related interest:

Breaking Free: A Recovery Workbook for Facing Codependence,
by Pia Mellody and Andrea Wells Miller